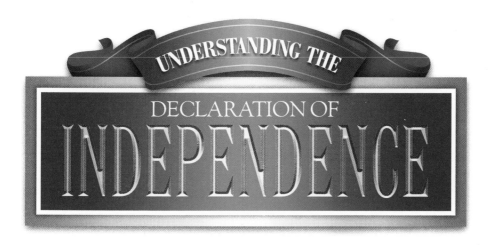

UNDERSTANDING THE DECLARATION OF INDEPENDENCE

WRITTEN BY SALLY SENZELL ISAACS

Published in 2012 by Dalmatian Press, LLC,
Franklin, Tennessee 37068-2068. 1-866-418-2572. Printed in China.

LEVEL **3** READER
READING LEVEL · GRADES 2 TO 4

Originally produced for Crabtree Publishing Company by Bender Richardson White, U.K.
Editor-in-Chief: Lionel Bender; Editor: Kelley MacAulay; Consultant: Professor Richard Jensen
Photographs: © Art Archive: Chateau de Berancourt/Gianni Dagli Orti: p. 16; © Corbis: Bettmann: p. 24;
© iStockphoto.com: p. 19 (both), 23; © Library of Congress: p. 8, 18 (ppmsa 08314);
© Northwind Picture Archives: p. 2, 3, 4, 5, 6, 7, 9, 10, 11, 12, 13, 14, 15, 20, 21, 22;
© Photos.com: p. 17
CE 14926/1211

A Big Step

The Declaration of Independence is one of the most important writings in the history of the United States. It was written and signed more than 235 years ago in 1776. Before that time, there was no country called the United States of America. There were 13 American colonies that belonged to Britain. The people in the colonies were British subjects. They followed laws made in Britain.

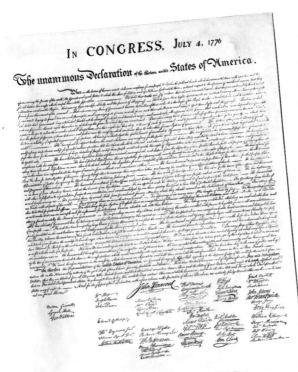

◄ *The Declaration of Independence was written on parchment paper, which was made from animal skin.*

A BIG DECISION

In 1776, the American colonies declared their independence. That means they told King George III of Britain that they did not want to be part of his country. They wanted to start a country of their own. The men who signed the Declaration took a big risk. Would the king punish them? Would they be able to build a new country on their own?

▼ *This map shows the land claims of the thirteen colonies established by England in 1763.*

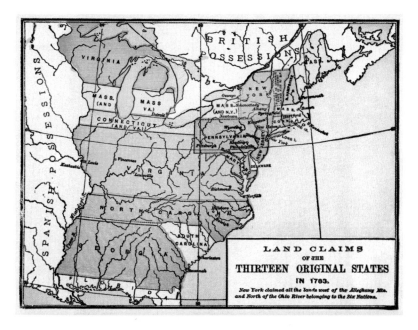

LIFE IN THE COLONIES

Around 1600, some Europeans moved to America and created the colonies. Many of them moved to the colonies for a better life. They wanted freedom that they did not have in Europe. They wanted a chance to own land and practice their own religions. In the colonies, most people lived on small farms. They had pigs and cows. They grew their own food, and chose their own leaders. People who lived in the colonies were called colonists.

Slaves

Many people did not choose to come to the colonies—they were forced to come. These people were slaves. A slave is owned by another person and is made to work for little or no pay.

RULED BY BRITAIN

The country of Britain was in charge of the 13 colonies. Even though Britain was very far away from the colonies, the colonists had to follow Britain's laws. They also had to pay taxes to Britain. A tax is money that people pay the government to run their country. King George III sent soldiers and officials to the colonies. They made sure the colonists obeyed the laws and paid the taxes.

◀ *George III was Britain's king from 1760 to 1820.*

The Terrible Taxes

By 1765, many colonists grew unhappy with Britain. The trouble was taxes! Britain needed money. It had fought a war with France that cost a lot of money. Britain's lawmakers, called the Parliament, wanted the colonists to pay for part of that war. Therefore, Parliament voted to make the colonists pay extra taxes on every-day items such as tea and cloth.

◀ *In local stores, colonists had to pay more money for their cloth, newspapers, sugar, and tea because of Britain's taxes.*

NO REPRESENTATION

The new taxes made the colonists angry. They felt that they should decide what taxes to pay, not people in Britain. The lawmakers in Parliament were representatives of the British people. People choose representatives to speak for them when laws are made. The colonists did not have representatives in Parliament to speak for them.

▼ *These colonists formed a group called the Sons of Liberty. They were angry about "taxation without representation."*

THE COLONIES ACT

The colonists were angry about *"taxation without representation."* Many of them stopped buying British tea. They made their own cloth instead of buying cloth from British stores. They wrote letters to the king. The letters said the taxes were unfair. King George III continued to tax the colonists, however.

Boston Tea Party
One night in 1773, some colonists, dressed as Native Americans, climbed onto a British ship in Boston Harbor. They threw boxes of tea into the water and ruined the tea so nobody could sell it. The incident became known as the Boston Tea Party. The king  was angry! He closed the Boston Harbor so that no ships could deliver goods until the colonists paid for the lost tea.

LOOKING FOR A BETTER WAY

On September 5, 1774, each colony sent representatives to a meeting at Carpenters' Hall in Philadelphia. The meeting was called the First Continental Congress. It was a type of Parliament. The representatives were all men. They hoped to find a way to get along with Britain. They met several times. They sent more letters to King George III. They also asked colonists to stop buying British goods.

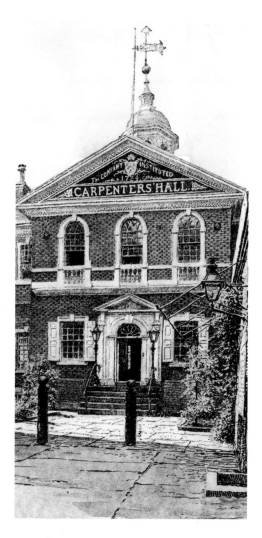

▲ *This is Carpenters' Hall, Philadelphia, where the First Congress was held.*

War Begins!

There was little hope to work things out with King George III. On April 19, 1775, British soldiers headed to the villages of Lexington and Concord, Massachusetts. They heard that colonial soldiers were collecting guns and gunpowder. The colonial soldiers called themselves minutemen because they could be ready to fight in a minute. No one knows who fired first, but soon a battle was raging.

An American Leader

A Second Continental Congress met and decided to form an American army. They chose a man to be the general in charge of the new army. His name was George Washington.

◄ *Washington was a respected leader of the Continental Army. He was later elected to be the first President of the United States.*

▲ *In the battle at Lexington, about 70 minutemen fought against almost 700 British soldiers.*

THE BRITISH ARE COMING

When the British soldiers arrived in Lexington, the minutemen met them with their guns. Before long, eight minutemen were dead. This was the first battle of a very bloody war between the colonists and Britain. The war lasted for six years. It is called the Revolutionary War or the American Revolution. A revolution is a strong move by people to change their government. A government is a group of leaders who run a country.

TALK OF INDEPENDENCE

Every day, more colonists turned against the king. They wanted to break away from Britain and start their own country. Colonists who fought for independence from Britain were called Patriots.

IN SECRET

On November 9, 1775, the men in Congress signed a Resolution of Secrecy. They promised to keep their plans a secret. It said that anyone who broke the promise must leave Congress as *"an enemy to the liberties of America."*

▶ *Patriot Patrick Henry made a speech exclaiming, "Give me liberty or give me death!"*

THE FAMOUS FIVE

By June 1776, the Continental Congress stopped writing letters to the king. Richard Henry Lee asked the Congress to vote on a statement saying "*these United Colonies are ... free and independent States.*" Congress voted yes. A group of five men started planning a Declaration of Independence.

The group was called the Committee of Five.

◄ *The Committee of Five were (left to right) Benjamin Franklin, Thomas Jefferson, Roger Sherman, John Adams, and Robert R. Livingston.*

Jefferson's Job

The Committee of Five asked Thomas Jefferson to write the first draft of the Declaration. Jefferson was a talented lawyer from Virginia. He wanted to help create a government that protects the rights of its people.

It took Jefferson 17 days to write the Declaration of Independence. He wanted colonists to hear the words and agree that it was time for independence from Britain. He wanted the king—and the rest of the world—to realize why the colonies were breaking away.

▲ *Jefferson (standing) discussed his ideas with Franklin and Adams before writing them down with quill and ink.*

Jefferson's Reasons for Independence
- The king has been unfair to the colonists.
- People have rights that cannot be taken away by kings.
- A government should protect the people's rights.
- A government should listen to its people.

GOD-GIVEN RIGHTS

The most famous words of the Declaration are *"We hold these truths to be self-evident that all men are created equal."*

Jefferson wrote that God gave rights to everyone. These are rights to life and liberty and the right to find happiness. Liberty is another word for "freedom."

The Declaration says that a government should make sure that people have these rights. Jefferson believed that people should create the government. People should choose their leaders and their laws.

A Long Wait for Equality

Jefferson had written about freedom for everyone. At the time of the Declaration, women, Native Americans, and African Americans were not granted the same rights as white men. For example, they could not vote for colonial leaders. They didn't enjoy those rights for many more years.

FAILED BY BRITAIN

▲ *British soldiers arrived by ship in New York.*

In the Declaration, Congress wanted to explain how King George III was hurting the colonists. King George III had stopped the colonies from trading with other countries, and prevented colonists from making decisions on many things in their towns. He had sent soldiers to punish the colonists who spoke against him. The soldiers burned down homes and other buildings.

TRYING TIMES

The king also forced the colonists to let the British soldiers live in their houses. He even paid soldiers from Germany to go to the colonies to fight the Patriots. At the same time, there were the king's high taxes! The Declaration says that the king *"destroyed the lives of our people."*

Then Jefferson explained that the colonists had really tried to work things out. They had sent many letters. They had asked the British people for help. However, the British people and the king were *"deaf to the voice of justice."*

◄ *In Boston, some Patriots were so angry that they caught British tax collectors and covered them in tar and feathers to protest against King George III and his laws.*

FREE STATES

What happens when a government is very unfair to its people? What if it will not change its ways? Jefferson believed that in these situations people have the right to bring about change. In the Declaration, he wrote that people have a right to start a new government that can give them *"safety and happiness."* This is what the Patriots were fighting for.

▶ *This is the Declaration of Independence that was drafted by Jefferson. There are many areas where he crossed out text while trying to write a version that everyone would accept.*

CLAIMING INDEPENDENCE

In the last part of the Declaration of Independence, Jefferson declared that the colonies were no longer part of Britain. He wrote that *"these United Colonies are...free and independent states."* They had the power to do everything that independent states had a right to do, such as creating their own laws and government. Finally, at the end of the Declaration, the colonies pledged to unite, or join together, and help one another. Here, Jefferson used the words *"United States of America"* for the first time.

▲ *In 1775, Congress met in the State House in Philadelphia, later called Independence Hall, the original home of the Liberty Bell.*

▲ *One of the first United States flags had 13 stars and 13 stripes to represent the 13 colonies.*

An Important Vote

On June 28, 1776, Jefferson finished writing the Declaration. On July 1, Congress met to vote on whether it would accept the document and declare independence. Some representatives asked to have one part of the Declaration crossed out before they would accept it. The part they wanted crossed out said that the king was wrong to allow slavery. Many of them owned slaves, so they would not agree to this. On July 2, representatives stood up one by one to say "yes" to independence. Then the document was neatly written with the new wording.

◄ *New Yorkers who wanted independence pulled down a statue of King George III.*

▲ *John Trumball painted this picture of the Committee of Five as they presented the Declaration to Congress.*

THE U.S.A. IS BORN

The final wording of the Declaration was approved two days later on July 4. A new country was born called the United States of America. The people were called Americans. That day, John Hancock, the president of the Congress, and Charles Thomson, Congress secretary, signed the Declaration. Later, the rest of the 56 men signed it, too. They were all very brave. If America lost the Revolution, the king would likely punish them.

Spread the Word!

America was independent! It was time to share the news with the colonists. After the approval on July 4, the Declaration was given to John Dunlap. He was a printer in Philadelphia. Dunlap worked through the night. He made copies of the Declaration on his printing presses. Messengers brought copies to soldiers fighting the war. They brought other copies to the villages and towns. On July 8, the Declaration was read to the public for the first time. Americans celebrated when they heard the news.

▼ *People gathered to hear the reading of the Declaration of Independence.*

THE WORDS LIVE ON

The words of the Declaration of Independence have been quoted throughout history. In 1858, Abraham Lincoln spoke out against slavery. He said that the Declaration promised life, liberty, and happiness to all men equally. When Lincoln became president of the United States, he ended slavery.

In 1848, Elizabeth Cady Stanton and others wrote a declaration for women's rights. The first part of it said, *"all men and women are created equal."*

Today, all Americans are free people. They choose their leaders and lawmakers. They are free to speak out against their government. The people can work together to make changes for the better.

◀ *Across America, people celebrate Independence Day every July 4.*

THE DECLARATION TODAY

Twenty-five of the first copies of the Declaration of Independence still exist today. The signed document is sealed under glass in Washington, D.C. It sits in a building called the National Archives. The air and temperature under the glass are set to preserve the special paper. Every year, millions of visitors come to see the Declaration that gave birth to liberty and our nation.

▼ *People are welcome to view the Declaration of Independence in the National Archives building in Washington, D.C.*